SAMUEL TAYLOR COLERIDGE was born in 1772, son of a vicar. He published verses as early as 1793, and in 1794 wrote, with Robert Southey, *The Fall of Robespierre*. In 1795 he made the acquaintance of William Wordsworth, and the two poets became fast friends. In 1798 they published *Lyrical Ballads*, which included Coleridge's "The Rime of the Ancient Mariner." This book, which represented a rejection of the artificial literary styles of the day in favor of the utmost simplicity of subject and style, was most unfavorably received. Coleridge's best-known poems, "The Ancient Mariner," "Christabel," and "Kubla Khan" are all mysterious in tone and implication. He also published influential works of literary theory and criticism. He died in 1834.

"For the space of two or three brief years, Coleridge's wings are spread and he touches the heights of Parnassus—he writes 'The Rime of the Ancient Mariner,' 'Christabel,' and 'Kubla Khan.'... He was visited by a poetic afflatus, an inspired state of mind in which the words came as come they must. Such is the state of inspiration, and such is the state of origination."

Sir Herbert Read

THE RIME
OF THE
ANCIENT MARINER

Samuel Taylor Coleridge

supplementary material by

Walter S. Hallenborg

 A BARD BOOK/PUBLISHED BY AVON BOOKS

AVON BOOKS
A division of
The Hearst Corporation
959 Eighth Avenue
New York, New York 10019

Copyright © 1967 by Avon Books
Published by arrangement with Avon Books
ISBN: 0-380-00999-4

First Bard Printing, October, 1967
Fifth Printing

BARD TRADEMARK REG. U.S. PAT. OFF. AND
FOREIGN COUNTRIES, REGISTERED TRADEMARK—
MARCA REGISTRADA, HECHO EN CHICAGO, U.S.A.

Printed in the U.S.A.

CONTENTS

THE LIFE OF
SAMUEL TAYLOR COLERIDGE

After his death in July of 1834, the autopsy revealed that Samuel Taylor Coleridge had suffered from a greatly enlarged heart and liver and that he had cysts on his lungs. This condition, according to Kathleen Coburn, may well have been one of the governing facts of Coleridge's life from about 1795.

We know that shortly before this he began to take laudanum, a tincture of opium, in order to relieve the pain of illness. We know, too, that he became addicted to opium, and that the addiction eventually contributed to the decline of his creative genius.

What sort of man was this? How shall we picture him? Here is his self-portrait: "As to me, my face, unless animated by immediate eloquence, expresses great sloth, and great, indeed, almost idiotic good nature. 'Tis a mere carcass of a face; fat, flabby, and expressive chiefly of inexpression . . . my shape, 'tis a good enough shape if measured, but my gait is awkward and the walk . . . indicates indolence capable of energies. . . .I cannot breathe through my nose, so my mouth, with sensual thick lips, is almost always open. In conversation I am impassioned, and oppose what I deem error with an eagerness which is often mistaken for personal asperity; but I am ever so swallowed up in the *thing* [the topic of discussion] that I perfectly forget my opponent. Such am I." (E. K. Chambers, pp. 65–66.)

Coleridge was born at Ottery St. Mary, Devonshire, England, on October 21, 1772. It was typical of him that he was not even sure of the date of his birth.

He was the youngest child of John Coleridge, a cleric who managed to have two wives and fourteen children. Very little is known of Ann Bowdon, Coleridge's mother. She is assumed to have been devoted to the care of the home and children, but with little taste for art or philosophy.

It was from his father, then, that Coleridge developed an interest in religion, philosophy, and artistic expression. There apparently was an intellectual affinity between the boy and the man. The Reverend Coleridge died when Samuel was nine.

Throughout his early youth the boy had been alienated and "different" from his older siblings. He grew up moody and alone. After the death of his father, he was sent to a famous free school, Christ's Hospital, which was located in the heart of London. At this school he met Charles Lamb, who was to be his friend for life. It was also where Samuel came under the instructional discipline of the Reverend James Boyer. This stern but apparently successful teacher gave the boy a firm foundation in classical studies and a taste for scholarship. He also fought Coleridge's introversion and indolence: "Boy! the School is your father! The School is your mother! The School is your sister—your brother—all the rest of your relations. Let's have no more crying." (Chambers, p. 10.) One can sense the zeal with which the Rev. Boyer pursued his calling.

At sixteen, Coleridge fell in love with the sister of a schoolmate. Mary Evans was her name, and it may be said that he was very serious about her until their breakup some six years later. He loved this girl, but he eventually married Sara Fricker, a girl for whom he was not suited (1795).

He had entered Jesus College at Cambridge in 1791 on a scholarship. His personal problems overwhelmed him, however, and he ran off to join the 15th Light Dragoons, using the name Silas Tomkyn Comberbacke.

10

Military service and horsemanship were clearly not the appropriate life for this nonathletic scholar, and it was not long before his family was able to win his dismissal. He returned to Cambridge but eventually abandoned his studies there.

In June of 1794, Coleridge met Robert Southey. With this more durable, less talented friend, Coleridge hatched an idea for an ideal society. They called it "Pantisocracy." The plan called for couples to live in a communal organization based on social ethics, religious freedom, and shared responsibility. Liberal education was to be a keystone of the plan. Twelve couples were to set up this colony on the banks of the Susquehanna River in Pennsylvania. It was a wild scheme that never came to anything.

The year 1797 has been called an *annus mirabilis* for Coleridge. His close friendship with William and Dorothy Wordsworth began early that year. The latter, Wordsworth's devoted sister, kept a journal of their experiences together, thereby giving the world a priceless insight into their lives.

Each poet proved to be the catalyst for the release of the other's greatness, Coleridge eventually producing *The Rime of the Ancient Mariner,* "Christabel," "Kubla Khan," and "France, An Ode." Together they published the *Lyrical Ballads,* which was a collection of their works. This book, not well received at the time, is now considered to be a landmark in the development of Romanticism.

In September, 1798, Coleridge, Wordsworth, and Dorothy went to Germany to learn the language, the literature, and the philosophy of that country. It was during this time that Coleridge came under the influence of the philosophy of Immanuel Kant.

Throughout most of his life, Coleridge sought to find a philosophical position which would undergird his Protestant faith. His conflict about immortality is expressed:

11

If dead, we cease to be; if total gloom
Swallow up life's brief flash for aye, we fare
As summer-gusts, of sudden birth and doom,
Whose sound and motion not alone declare,
But are their whole of being! If the breath
Be Life itself, and not its task and tent,
If even a soul like Milton's can know death;
O Man! thou vessel purposeless, unmeant,
Yet drone-hive strange of phantom purposes!
Surplus of Nature's dread activity,
Which, as she gazed on some nigh-finished vase,
Retreating slow, with meditative pause,
She formed with restless hands unconsciously,
Blank accident! nothing's anomaly!
   (From "Human Life—On the Denial of
   Immortality," 1817)

Kant's philosophy led Coleridge to the idea that the religious experience is one that is *felt* through *faith*, and that it is not a matter of understanding.

The turn of the century marked the beginning of Coleridge's decline as a poet. In 1802 he wrote (with great poetic skill) "Dejection: An Ode," in which he lamented the waning of his powers. At this time he had fallen in love with Sara Hutchinson, but his unhappy marriage was an effective obstacle to that relationship. In Coleridge's time, divorce was not an acceptable answer to marital problems.

The years 1804-1806 were spent in Malta. He made the voyage there in hope of finding a climate more suitable to his rheumatic condition. His experiences on that trip resulted in his making several revisions in *The Rime of the Ancient Mariner*. His original writing of the poem had been made entirely without benefit of direct experience with the sea.

His return to England must have been awkward for all concerned. He was reluctant to return to Mrs. Coleridge and to the circle of friends he had known. In 1807, he and his wife were formally separated.

The next eight years saw him doing some lecturing and publishing. In 1813, he produced his play, *Osario*, which had a successful run of twenty performances. During these years, it was characteristic of him to visit friends and end up staying for long periods of time. Finally, in 1816, he was taken into the home of Dr. and Mrs. James Gillman, remaining there for the eighteen years still left to him. One cannot underestimate the kindness of the Gillmans. They were, after all, taking in a man in ill health who was addicted to the use of opium. The Gillman home was located at Highgate, and Coleridge, who enjoyed the role of wise man of letters, became known as the "Sage of Highgate."

Biographia Literaria, which was both a literary history and a new direction in literary criticism, was published in 1817. The fact that it came to be written at all was partly due to the efforts of John Morgan, who wrote much of it from Coleridge's dictation. At this time, the poet was still deep in the grip of addiction. In the ensuing years, the Gillmans were able to help him control his intake of opium.

At the age of fifty-one Coleridge wrote these lines about himself:

I see these locks in silvery slips,
This drooping gait, this altered size:
But Spring-tide blossoms on thy lips,
And tears take sunshine from thine eyes!
Life is but thought: so I think I will
That Youth and I are house-mates still.
(From "Youth and Age," 1823)

Rheumatic fever had aged him prematurely but had not destroyed his spirit.

Coleridge died at age sixty-two on July 25, 1834.

Charles Lamb, his friend since the days at Christ's Hospital, and Wordsworth were among the few people who expressed a sense of great loss. Wordsworth commented: "I have known many men who have done wonderful things, but the only wonderful man I ever saw was Coleridge."

His wife, Sara, and their three children, Hartley, Sara, and Derwent, did not attend the funeral. Another son, Berkely, had died in infancy. On that occasion Coleridge had written: "On this strange, strange scene-shifter Death!—that giddies one with insecurity and so unsubstantiates the living things that one has grasped and handled!" (Chambers)

Many years later, in anticipation of his own demise, the poet wrote this epitaph:

Stop, Christian passerby! Stop, child of God,
And read with gentle breast. Beneath this sod
A poet lies, or that which once seemed he.
O, lift one thought in prayer for S. T. C.
That he who many a year with toil of breath
Found death in life, may here find life in death!
Mercy for praise—to be forgiven for fame
He asked, and hoped, through Christ. Do thou the
    same!

THE SIGNIFICANCE OF COLERIDGE

This disorganized, procrastinating giant of English literature won praise as a lecturer, journalist, conversationalist, theologian, philosopher, poet, and literary critic. It is in the last two categories that his true significance lies.

With Wordsworth, Coleridge is thought of as one of the founders of the romantic spirit in English literature. That spirit sought to emphasize the importance of the individual. It said, through literature, the same thing that was being expressed through the revolutionary and political movements in France and America.

The poets of the Romantic school sought to express the importance of the emotions and the imagination as they occur spontaneously in the individual. They sought to find God in nature.

John Livingston Lowes quotes Coleridge from *Biographia Literaria,* Chapter Fourteen. The organization of the quote throws light on the basic credo governing Romanticism and also explains Coleridge's thinking with respect to the writing of *The Rime of the Ancient Mariner:*

> During the first year that Mr. Wordsworth and I were neighbours, our conversations turned frequently on the two cardinal points of poetry, the power of exciting the sympathy of the reader by a faithful adherence to the truth of nature, and the power of giving the interest of novelty by the modifying colour of imagination. The sudden charm, which accident

of light and shade, which moon-light or sun-set diffused over known and familiar landscape, appeared to represent the practicability of combining both . . . and this idea originated the plan of the *Lyrical Ballads*; in which it was agreed, that my endeavours should be directed to persons and characters supernatural, or at least romantic; yet so as to transfer from our inward nature a human interest and semblance of truth sufficient to procure for these shadows of imagination that willing suspension of disbelief for the moment which constitutes poetic faith . . . with this view I wrote the *Ancient Mariner*. (Lowes, *The Road to Xanadu*, p. 295)

In the field of literary criticism Coleridge's influence is also of fundamental importance. He is generally credited with being the founder of modern literary criticism. In this regard, John Stuart Mill referred to him as one of the seminal minds of the period. Coleridge's approach to criticism is discussed by W. W. Robson in the *Concise Encyclopedia of English and American Poets and Poetry*, edited by Spender and Hall:

The critic who most deserves to be called the founder of modern criticism is Coleridge . . . Johnson (Samuel) can show sensitivity as well as his characteristic incisiveness; but his analysis even at its best has not the peculiar inwardness of Coleridge . . . And it is this inwardness, obviously related to Coleridge's preoccupation with psychology, which characterizes his best criticism . . . Coleridge is to be honoured as the first great practitioner of "close analysis." (pp. 106–108)

In summary then, we may think of Coleridge's significance in these two major ways: His influence upon the Romantic movement in English literature, and his influence on literary criticism. Such a summary cannot begin to do justice to him. There has been a tremendous amount of scholarly interest in him. We can only suggest that the ambitious reader search further for more complete studies.

THE STRUCTURE AND SPECIAL QUALITIES OF *The Rime of the Ancient Mariner*

1. The poem consists of seven parts. There is a kind of supernatural significance to the number seven. We recall, for example, what the Bible teaches about the creation of the world.

2. The poem is cyclic in nature in that the Mariner returns to his homeland at the end of the poem.

3. Coleridge used the old English ballad form which employs four line stanzas with a rhyme pattern a b c b. He varied this pattern when it suited his purpose.

4. The poem may be considered as straight narrative on a level of appreciation one might bring to the ballads of Robert W. Service ("The Cremation of Sam McGee," for example).

5. The poem may be appreciated for its marvelous magical qualities.

6. The poem may be appreciated for its rich use of symbolism. The symbolic meaning of the Albatross has been the subject of a considerable amount of scholarly speculation.

7. The poem may be thought of as an allegory on the Christian faith.

8. The reader may also speculate about the poem

as being an unconscious expression of the poet's problems as a human being. Various writers have seen possible Freudian implications in the work. In this vein, one might ask: Who is the Mariner really? Who is the woman on the skeleton ship? . . . and so on.

THE ANNOTATIONS AND COMMENTS

The editor has, of course, responded to *The Rime of the Ancient Mariner* as one individual. He has speculated about the meanings that lie within a noble poem. On occasion, he has turned to the thoughts of various scholars in order to enrich the reader's pleasure and understanding. The total effect to be hoped for is that the reader and the editor may enjoy the poem together, and that the reader will bring his own intellect and sensitivity to bear. Ultimately, the poem can only "happen" for each person as it strikes him.

The guide is not meant to supplement the responsibility of the reader as he voyages through the lines that the poet has set down. Many readers will want to carry the study of the poem beyond the modest limits of this edition. If they do, they will find a veritable treasure trove of scholarship devoted to it. They may then come to appreciate the extent to which this poem speaks to humanity.

The Wedding-Guest, anticipating the joy of the wedding, is confronted with a disturbing situation. Those of us who lead respectable lives are always upset when a derelict aggressively invades our complacent privacy. Now, abruptly, in a pleasurable festive setting appears this skinny, mysterious old sailor. (Notice how the words "old sailor" compare with "ancient Mariner." Coleridge's term has a poetic elegance about it, while the other has the prosaic ring of the commonplace.)

PART I

An ancient
Mariner
meeteth
three
Gallants
bidden
to a wedding
feast, and
detaineth
one.

It is an ancient Mariner
And he stoppeth one of three.
"By thy long grey beard and glittering eye,
Now wherefore stopp'st thou me?

The Bridegroom's doors are opened wide,   5
And I am next of kin;
The guests are met, the feast is set:
May'st hear the merry din?"

We can sense the Wedding-Guest's revulsion at the touch of the Mariner's hand.

"Eftsoons" means "at once." The poet uses archaic language to add to the strange and marvelous mood of the poem.

The hypnotic power of the Mariner might be likened to the power of the artist to hold our attention perhaps even against our will. Coleridge, a man of acute sensitivity, sought to communicate with his reader as the Mariner did with the Wedding-Guest.

He holds him with his skinny hand,
"There was a ship," quoth he.   10
"Hold off! unhand me greybeard loon!"
Eftsoons his hand dropt he.

*The
Wedding-
Guest is
spellbound
by the eye of
the old sea-
faring man,
and con-
strained to
hear his tale.*

He holds him with his glittering eye—
The Wedding-Guest stood still,
And listens like a three years' child: 15
The Mariner hath his will.

The Wedding-Guest sat on a stone:
He cannot choose but hear;
And thus spake on that ancient man,
The bright-eyed Mariner.   20

"Kirk" is a Scottish word meaning church.

In his marginal gloss, the poet refers to the "line." The line is the equator.

The Sun will prove to be an implacable enemy in this poem. The reader may want to compare the events which occur when the sun is shining, and those that occur when the moon is on high.

Martin Gardner (p. 42) points out that the weight of evidence sets the story as taking place in the Middle Ages. The reference to the bassoon would be an anachronism since this instrument did not exist at that time.

"The ship was cheered, the harbour cleared,
Merrily did we drop
Below the kirk, below the hill,
Below the lighthouse top.

The Sun came up upon the left,   25
Out of the sea came he!
And he shone bright, and on the right
Went down into the sea.

Higher and higher every day,
Till over the mast at noon—"   30
The Wedding-Guest he beat his breast,
For he heard the loud bassoon.

The bride hath paced into the hall,
Red as a rose is she:
Nodding their heads before her goes   35
The merry minstrelsy.

The Wedding-Guest continues to be troubled. His anxiety stems now from the nature of the tale he is hearing as well as from the fact that the wedding is proceeding without him.

We may wonder about the symbolic meaning of the storm. Does man in his quest for life deliberately put himself into situations that force him to flee in dread?

This is the first time that the poet departs from the regular ballad rhyme scheme, which is a b c b.

The poetic impact of the expanded stanza is enhanced by the regularity of the four-line stanzas preceding it.

The Wedding-Guest he beat his breast,
Yet he cannot choose but hear;
And thus spake on that ancient man,
The bright-eyed Mariner.   40

*The ship
driven by a
storm toward
the south
pole.*

"And now the STORM-BLAST came and he
Was tyrannous and strong:
He struck with his o'ertaking wings,
And chased us south along.

With sloping masts and dipping prow,   45
As who pursued with yell and blow
Still treads the shadow of his foe,
And forward bends his head,
The ship drove fast, loud roared the blast,
And southward aye we fled.   50

John Livingston Lowes set himself the task of tracing the sources Coleridge used in order to produce *The Rime of the Ancient Mariner. The Road to Xanadu*, a tremendous piece of literary detective work, was the result. One chapter is devoted to the fields of ice. Apparently, Coleridge had read extensively in various travel books of the time. Lowes quotes a number of authors who had sailed the Arctic seas (p. 146): "this hell of ice . . . a frightful rumbling, and cracking of the ice as if many cannons had been fired at once . . . and then ensued a violent noise like the roaring of a cascade . . . caused the ice to part in an astonishing manner, rending and cracking with a tremendous noise, surpassing that of the loudest thunder."

"cracked and growled, and roared and howled,"—a good example of the poetic device called *onomatopoeia*.

And now there came both mist and snow,
And it grew wondrous cold:
And ice, mast-high, came floating by,
As green as emerald.

And through the drifts the snowy clifts   55
Did send a dismal sheen:
Nor shapes of men nor beasts we ken—
The ice was all between.

The ice was here, the ice was there,
The ice was all around: 60
It cracked and growled, and roared and howled,
Like noises in a swound!

Many scholars have pondered the symbolic meaning of the Albatross. Coleridge's reference to its being like a Christian soul has been expanded upon. Some have seen the bird as symbolizing Christ himself. Other interpretations have asserted that Coleridge was thinking of the creative imagination of the artist. In this view, the poem becomes a personal record of the artist's conflict with himself. Others have seen the Albatross as the symbol of the qualities of love and trust. John Livingston Lowes saw it as the pivotal and unifying element in the poem. Around this point of focus, the other elements in the poem proceed.

Till a great sea-bird, called the Albatross, came through the snow-fog, and was received with great joy and hospitality.

At length did cross an Albatross,
Through the fog it came;
As if it had been a Christian soul,   65
We hailed it in God's name.

It ate the food it ne'er had eat,
And round and round it flew.
The ice did split with a thunder-fit;
The helmsman steered us through!   70

And lo! the Albatross proveth a bird of good omen, and followeth the ship as it returned northward through fog and floating ice.

And a good south wind sprung up behind;
The Albatross did follow,
And every day, for food or play,
Came to the mariner's hollo!

The shooting of the Albatross with a "cross"-bow raises thoughts of a crucifixion. The Albatross has come as a sign of the grace of God . . . the Mariner (mankind) renounces God's love and murders it . . . there is no cause for the act other than the iniquity existing in the human heart.

E. M. W. Tillyard (p. 484) writes, "The act could be interpreted as the essential act of devilment, the act of pride, of the unbridled assertion of the self."

Robert Penn Warren (p. 229) writes: "The crime is, symbolically, a murder, and a particularly heinous murder, for it involves the violation of hospitality and of gratitude . . . and of sanctity."

In mist or cloud, on mast or shroud,   75
It perched for vespers nine;
Whiles all the night, through fog-smoke white,
Glimmered the white moon-shine."

*The ancient
Mariner in-
hospitably
killeth the
pious bird of
good omen.*

"God save thee, ancient Mariner!
From the fiends, that plague thee thus!—   80
Why look'st thou so?"—With my cross-bow
I shot the Albatross.

This stanza is an echo of lines 25–29 in Part I. The movements of the sun are opposite because, of course, the ship is now sailing northward.

Despite the supernatural and imaginative quality of the poem, Coleridge held it within the bounds of geographical realism. According to Lowes, Coleridge had in mind that the ship had now rounded Cape Horn and was proceeding northward into the Pacific Ocean.

PART II

The Sun now rose upon the right:
Out of the sea came he,
Still hid in mist, and on the left   85
Went down into the sea.

And the good south wind still blew behind,
But no sweet bird did follow,
Nor any day for food or play
Came to the mariners' hollo!   90

The Mariner has not yet begun to pay for the crime of killing the Albatross, but the scene is being set. When the rest of the crew approves of the killing, God (symbolized by the sun) is ready to carry out his punishment.

Repetition of the "f" sound is an example of *alliteration*.

His ship-
mates cry out
against the
ancient Mar-
iner, for kill-
ing the bird
of good luck.

And I had done a hellish thing,
And it would work 'em woe:
For all averred, I had killed the bird
That made the breeze to blow.
Ah wretch! said they, the bird to slay,   95
That made the breeze to blow!

But when
the fog
cleared off,
they justify
the same,
and thus
make them-
selves accom-
plices in the
crime.

Nor dim nor red, like God's own head,
The glorious Sun uprist:
Then all averred, I had killed the bird
That brought the fog and mist.   100
'Twas right, said they, such birds to slay,
That bring the fog and mist.

The fair
breeze con-
tinues; the
ship enters
the Pacific
Ocean, and
sails north-
ward, even
till it reaches
the Line.

The fair breeze blew, the white foam flew,
The furrow followed free;
We were the first that ever burst   105
Into that silent sea.

God's punishment begins. We can anticipate the inferno, the true hell to be visited upon the Mariner and the crew. If the poet has created a symbolic hell, will he show us a means for gaining release from hell?

The position of the sun indicates that the ship has returned to the equator. (Refer to line 30.)

The ship
hath been
suddenly
becalmed.

Down dropt the breeze, the sails dropt down,
'Twas sad as sad could be;
And we did speak only to break
The silence of the sea!   110

All in a hot and copper sky,
The bloody Sun, at noon,
Right up above the mast did stand,
No bigger than the Moon.

E. M. W. Tillyard (p. 485) quotes Lowes and continues with his own comment. Lowes: "The sequence which follows the Mariner's initial act accomplishes two ends: it unifies and credibilizes the poem . . . the train of cause and consequence is more than a consolidating factor of the poem. It happens to be life, as every human being knows it. You do a foolish or an evil deed, and its results come home to you."

Tillyard: " . . . it is precisely the blend of sheer truth to human experience with the narrative power, the fantastic happenings, and the brilliant pictures, that makes *The Ancient Mariner* so rich and so inspiring."

Robert Penn Warren (p. 202) also quotes Lowes with reference to the idea that Coleridge wanted as his theme "some interest deeply human." "This interest deeply human turns out to be the idea of transgression and absolution, and of the train of consequence which persists even after absolution. . . . "

Day after day, day after day,   115
We stuck, nor breath nor motion;
As idle as a painted ship
Upon a painted ocean.

And the Albatross begins to be avenged.

Water, water, everywhere,
And all the boards did shrink;   120
Water, water, everywhere,
Nor any drop to drink.

Martin Gardner (p. 56) points out that Coleridge is echoing Shakespeare in *Macbeth* (Act I, Scene 3):

The weird sisters, hand in hand,
Posters of the sea and land,
Thus do go about, about.

Gardner goes on to say: "The chant occurs just after one of the witches has pronounced a curse on a mariner, depriving him of drink and sleep, and sending a storm to wreck his ship."

Oscar Wilde created devilish dances in *The Ballad of Reading Gaol* that remind us of Coleridge's stanza. Some examples:

With slouch and swing around the ring
We trod the Fools' parade

and

About, about, in ghastly rout
They trod a saraband;

or

Around, around, they waltzed and wound;
Some wheeled in smirking pairs;

In his reference to death-fires dancing, Coleridge may have had in mind the maritime phenomenon known as "St. Elmo's fire."

The very deep did rot: O Christ!
That ever this should be!
Yea, slimy things did crawl with legs   125
Upon the slimy sea.

About, about, in reel and rout
The death-fires danced at night;
The water, like a witch's oils,
Burnt green, and blue and white.   130

With reference to Coleridge's marginal gloss: These invisible inhabitants were called daemons (not to be confused with demons). The daemons were intermediaries between gods and men. Coleridge had read Michael Psellus who was an enthusiastic writer in this field. Coleridge had also planned to write "The Wanderings of Cain" with Wordsworth. He had therefore been reading Josephus. The latter was a Jewish historian who lived shortly after the time of Christ. Josephus' account of the Essenes dealt with departed souls.

The ancient Mariner is deprived of his right to wear the symbol of devotion to Christ; he must wear the symbol of his sin. Thus the word "albatross" has come to signify a burden or a curse.

The reader will note that each of the first six parts of the poem end with some reference to the killing of the Albatross.

A Spirit had followed them; one of the invisible inhabitants of this planet, neither departed souls nor angels; concerning whom the

And some in dreams assurèd were
Of the Spirit that plagued us so;
Nine fathom deep he had followed us
From the land of mist and snow.

And every tongue, through utter drought,   135
Was withered at the root;
We could not speak, no more than if
We had been choked with soot.

learned Jew, Josephus, and the Platonic Constantinopolitan, Michael Psellus, may be consulted. They are very numerous, and there is no climate or element without one or more.

The ship-mates, in their sore distress, would fain throw

Ah! well a-day! what evil looks
Had I from old and young!   140
Instead of the cross, the Albatross
About my neck was hung.

the whole guilt on the ancient Mariner: in sign whereof they hang the dead sea-bird round his neck.

Coleridge repeats the word weary four times. The effect drains the sensitive reader. The closing lines of the stanza raise the hope that some form of help is on the way.

The poet brings the ship to us slowly and the suspense builds.

"Wist" is the past tense and past participle of the archaic verb wit, which meant to know.

PART III

There passed a weary time. Each throat
Was parched, and glazed each eye.
A weary time! a weary time!   145
How glazed each weary eye,
When looking westward, I beheld
A something in the sky.

The ancient Mariner beholdeth a sign in the element afar off.

At first it seemed a little speck,
And then it seemed a mist;   150
It moved and moved, and took at last
A certain shape, I wist.

A speck, a mist, a shape, I wist!
And still it neared and neared:
As if it dodged a water-sprite,   155
It plunged and tacked and veered.

We can accept Coleridge's gloss which says that the Mariner needed the moisture of his own blood in order to be able to speak. If we return to Christian symbolism, then the biting of the arm becomes a reference to the sacrifices of body and blood as a means of winning redemption. Perhaps the Mariner has begun to pay for his sins in religious terms. At this point he has not won salvation.

"Gramercy" means great thanks. In his gloss Coleridge might have said that they gasped as they watched.

Lowes (p. 274) discusses Part III: "The most dramatic of the seven sections . . . is the third, in which the spectre bark comes onward without wind or tide, pauses, and shoots away. Now the spectre bark is the 'skeleton ship with figures in it,' of Cruikshank's 'strange dream.' So much we know of Wordsworth's testimony." (In 1843 Wordsworth reported that *The Ancient Mariner* had been based on a dream experienced by Coleridge's friend, Cruikshank.)

At its nearer approach, it seemeth him to be a ship; and at a dear ransom he freeth his speech from the bonds of thirst.

With throats unslaked, with black lips baked,
We could nor laugh nor wail;
Through utter drought all dumb we stood!
I bit my arm, I sucked the blood,   160
And cried, A sail! a sail!

With throats unslaked, with black lips baked,
Agape they heard me call:
A flash of joy;
Gramercy! they for joy did grin,
And all at once their breath drew in,   165
As they were drinking all.

And horror follows. For can it be a ship that comes on-ward without wind or tide?

See! see! (I cried) she tacks no more!
Hither to work us weal;
Without a breeze, without a tide,
She steadies with upright keel!   170

51

As the spectre bark nears we reach a deeper stage of unreality. Tillyard (p. 487) discusses degrees of nearness to reality: "The harbor town, occurring in a narrative, is less real than the wedding-guest and the wedding, but more 'real' than the realms visited in the voyage; and these degrees of reality can hardly be without their effect."

We are now in a reddened purgatory-like setting awaiting the spectre bark; surely we have reached the limits of the supernatural, the unreal.

"Gossamer": a fine filmy cobweb, seen on grass and bushes, or floating in the air in calm weather, especially in autumn. Reference is made to goose summer, or Indian summer, the time when goose was eaten, also the time when plant life carried this filmy cobweb. (See *American College Dictionary* entry.)

The western wave was all a-flame.
The day was well nigh done!
Almost upon the western wave
Rested the broad bright Sun;
When that strange shape drove suddenly   175
Betwixt us and the Sun.

It seemeth him but the skeleton of a ship.

And straight the Sun was flecked with bars,
(Heaven's Mother send us grace!)
As if through a dungeon-grate he peered
With broad and burning face.   180

And its ribs are seen as bars on the face of the setting Sun.

Alas! (thought I, and my heart beat loud)
How fast she nears and nears!
Are those *her* sails that glance in the Sun,
Like restless gossameres?

John Livingston Lowes' *The Road to Xanadu* is the pre-eminent source with reference to the sources Coleridge used to write *The Ancient Mariner*. We turn to him again (p. 277). "There is an ancient tale, which belongs to the oral tradition of the Netherlands, of one Falkenburg, who, for murder done, is doomed to wander forever on the sea, accompanied by two spectral forms, one white, one black . . . And in a ship with all sails set, the two forms play at dice for the wanderer's soul. 'Six hundred years has that ship been sailing without either helm or helmsman, and so long have the two been playing for . . . his soul.' (Thorpe, *Northern Mythology* III) A tale then, of two spectral figures casting dice on a phantom ship for the soul of an eternal wanderer was current on the seas. One thing is clear: somehow . . . the story had reached Coleridge, and merged with Cruikshank's dream."

Are those *her* ribs through which the Sun 185
Did peer, as through a grate?
And is that Woman all her crew?
Is that a Death? and are there two?
Is Death that woman's mate?

Her lips were red, *her* looks were free, 190
Her locks were yellow as gold:
Her skin was as white as leprosy,
The Night-mare LIFE-IN-DEATH was she,
Who thicks man's blood with cold.

The naked hulk alongside came, 195
And the twain were casting dice;
"The game is done! I've won! I've won!"
Quoth she, and whistles thrice.

In equatorial latitudes the earth bulks larger. As the earth spins away from the setting sun, this greater bulk brings night more suddenly; also, the speed of the earth's rotation is greatest at the equator. Note the effectiveness of "at one stride comes the dark" (*personification*).

"looked sideways up" may cause the reader to think of a dog slinking away in abject fear . . . a powerful way to depict the fears of the men.

No twilight within the courts of the Sun.

The Sun's rim dips; the stars rush out:
At one stride comes the dark;   200
With far-heard whisper, o'er the sea,
Off shot the spectre-bark.

At the rising of the Moon,

We listened and looked sideways up!
Fear at my heart, as at a cup,
My life-blood seemed to sip!   205
The stars were dim, and thick the night,
The steersman's face by his lamp gleamed
      white;
From the sails the dew did drip—
Till clomb above the eastern bar
The hornèd Moon, with one bright star   210
Within the nether tip.

H. A. Bates in his notes (p. 20) quotes Coleridge: "It is a common superstition among sailors that something is going to happen when stars dog the moon."

Gardner (p. 68) augments the reader's appreciation of this stanza: "The repetition of 'one by one' suggests that one at a time each sailor stares at the dying moon, turns his eyes upon the Mariner, and drops lifeless to the deck."

A religious interpretation of a life of sin and selfishness might be a form of living death.

The religious impulse has also tended to give substance to the soul. Bates (p. 21) directs us to some lines from Rossetti's "Sister Helen":

Ah! what is this that sighs in the frost?
A soul that's lost as mine is lost.

One after another,

One after one, by the star-dogged Moon,
Too quick for groan or sigh,
Each turned his face with a ghastly pang,
And cursed me with his eye.   215

His ship-mates drop down dead.

Four times fifty living men,
(And I heard nor sigh nor groan)
With heavy thump, a lifeless lump,
They dropped down one by one.

But Life-in-Death begins her work on the ancient Mariner.

The souls did from their bodies fly,—   220
They fled to bliss or woe!
And every soul, it passed me by,
Like the whizz of my cross-bow!

Coleridge acknowledged that Wordsworth wrote the last two lines of this stanza. The ribbed sea-sand is likened to the wrinkled flesh of the Mariner.

PART IV

*The Wed-
ding-Guest
feareth that a
Spirit is talk-
ing to him;*

"I fear thee, ancient Mariner!
I fear thy skinny hand!   225
And thou art long, and lank, and brown,
As is the ribbed sea-sand.

We have returned to the reality of the Wedding-Guest.

The complete isolation of the Mariner may be thought of as the product of his sinfulness, his selfishness. The repetition of the long "o" vowel in the word "alone" lends great power to the meaning and intent of the stanza.

With respect to these same lines, Martin Gardner (p. 70) quotes Thomas Wolfe. Wolfe wrote these lines to his former schoolteacher, Mary Roberts, in 1927: "I think I shall call it, 'Alone, Alone,' for the idea that broods over it, and in it, and behind it, is that we are all upon this earth we walk on—that naked and alone do we come into life, and alone, a stranger, each to each, we live upon it. The title, as you know, I have taken from the poem I love best, 'The Rime of the Ancient Mariner.'" Wolfe was referring to the novel which he eventually called *Look Homeward Angel*.

I fear thee and thy glittering eye,
And thy skinny hand, so brown."—
Fear not, fear not, thou Wedding-Guest! 230
This body dropt not down.

Alone, alone, all, all alone,
Alone on a wide wide sea!
And never a saint took pity on
My soul in agony. 235

But the ancient Mariner assureth him of his bodily life, and proceedeth to relate his horrible penance.

The reader may ponder the use of the word "beautiful" here. Perhaps the agony and contortion of the living face attains a kind of composed beauty in death. The Mariner likens himself to slimy things. Perhaps Coleridge likened himself to the Mariner.

The Mariner's inability to pray may be considered as an ultimate state of imprisonment. The act of prayer might be thought of as a positive and initiating desire to communicate; even if the person believes that he is sending his words out into an infinite void, it must still be said that he has made a positive effort to communicate; he has made a move toward love.

He despiseth the creatures of the calm,

The many men, so beautiful!
And they all dead did lie:
And a thousand thousand slimy things
Lived on; and so did I.

And envieth that they should live, and so many lie dead.

I looked upon the rotting sea,   240
And drew my eyes away;
I looked upon the rotting deck,
And there the dead men lay.

I looked to heaven, and tried to pray;
But or ever a prayer had gusht,   245
A wicked whisper came, and made
My heart as dry as dust.

Line 250 is anapestic in nature. It consists of four phrases, each of which has an anapestic form: two unstressed sounds followed by a stressed sound (or syllable).

Coleridge wrote the following jingle as a means of teaching the various forms of meter in poetry:

/—stressed syllable (long)
X—unstressed syllable (short)

"Metrical Feet: Lesson for a Boy"

```
 /   X /   X   / X /
Trochee trips from long to short;
 X  / X /   X / X  /
From long to long in solemn sort
  /  / X /   /   /   / / /
Slow Spondee stalks; strong foot! yet ill able
/ X X /   X X  / X X / X X
Ever to come up with Dactyl trisyllable
X/ X  /   X   / X /
Iambics march from short to long;—
  X X /  X X /   X X  / X X /
With a leap and a bound the swift Anapests throng.
 X / X X /   X  X  / X X  /
One syllable long with one short at each side,
X  /  X X /    X X / X /
Amphibrachys hastes with a stately stride.
```

I closed my lids, and kept them close,
And the balls like pulses beat;
For the sky and the sea, and the sea and the sky 250
Lay like a load on my weary eye,
And the dead were at my feet.

This stanza makes us question our interpretation of the use of the word "beautiful" in line 236.

Gardner (p. 70) speculates: "Perhaps Coleridge is thinking of a medieval superstition—an orphan's curse, like the curse of an old person, a dying person, a priest, a beggar, and so on, was regarded as unusually potent."

*But the curse
liveth for
him in the
eye of the
dead men.*

The cold sweat melted from their limbs,
Nor rot nor reek did they:
The look with which they looked on me   255
Had never passed away.

An orphan's curse would drag to hell
A spirit from on high;
But oh! more horrible than that
Is the curse in a dead man's eye!   260
Seven days, seven nights, I saw that curse,
And yet I could not die.

This stanza signals a change in mood; there is a calmness to this Moon; though the stars are with her, she is no longer star-dogged. The quiet ascent of the Moon augments the mood change.

The marginal gloss is a beautiful work of prose itself. Its length reminds us of some humorous and mildly critical lines written by Lord Byron in his long poem, *Don Juan:*

> And Coleridge too has lately taken wing,
> But like a hawk encumber'd with his hood,—
> Explaining metaphysics to the nation—
> I wish he would explain his Explanation.

Byron was referring to *Biographia Literaria* which Coleridge published in 1817.

The change in mood continues. Compare this description of the snakes with that in Part II. Perhaps beauty or horror is in the eye of the beholder. The change that has taken place is in the Mariner. He may be in the first stage of his redemption.

In his loneli-
ness and fix-
edness he
yearneth
towards the
journeying
Moon, and
the stars that
still sojourn,
yet still move
onward; and
everywhere
The moving Moon went up the sky,
And no where did abide:
Softly she was going up,   265
And a star or two beside—

Her beams bemocked the sultry main,
Like April hoar-frost spread;
But where the ship's huge shadow lay,
The charmèd water burnt alway   270
A still and awful red.

the blue sky belongs to them, and is their appointed rest, and their
native country and their own natural homes, which they enter un-
announced, as lords that are certainly expected and yet there is a
silent joy at their arrival.

By the light
of the Moon
he beholdeth
God's crea-
tures of the
great calm.
Beyond the shadow of the ship,
I watched the water-snakes:
They moved in tracks of shining white,
And when they reared, the elfish light   275
Fell off in hoary flakes.

Redemption can be thought of as a way of looking at life. The act of love states that the world is alive; salvation grows from a belief in the worthwhileness of life.

Discussing the stages of the redeeming process, Robert Penn Warren (p. 244) writes: "First, the recognition of happiness and beauty; second, love; third, the blessing of the creatures; fourth, freedom from the spell."

Within the shadow of the ship
I watched their rich attire:
Blue, glossy green, and velvet black,
They coiled and swam; and every track   280
Was a flash of golden fire.

In his book *How Does a Poem Mean?*, John Ciardi (p. 721) discusses the end of Part IV: "The Mariner breathes forth unawares a blessing upon the creatures of the deep and immediately the guilty weight of the Albatross falls from him and sinks 'like lead into the sea.'"

Students are often tempted to interpret this action as symbolizing the Mariner's forgiveness and release from pain. But to accept this interpretation is to ignore the words of the spirit at the end of Part V: "The man hath penance done, And penance more will do." The Mariner suffers when the Albatross is about his neck, and he continues to suffer when he is released from its weight. Obviously, however, the nature of his suffering has changed. Until love touches his soul he suffers in one way. As soon as love has touched him the mood changes: a sleep refreshes him and he wakens from it to a visitation and a whole new motion of events. The key to an understanding of this change lies in basic

*Their beauty
and their
happiness.*

*He blesseth
them in his
heart.*

O happy living things! no tongue
Their beauty might declare:
A spring of love gushed from my heart,
And I blessed them unaware: 285
Sure my kind saint took pity on me,
And I blessed them unaware.

Christian theology, in which love is the beginning of redemption. Until love touches the Mariner he has suffered as a damned soul suffers, without hope. As soon as love touches him his sufferings become a penance rather than a doom. Penance is a state of grace for, however painful it may be, it leads to salvation. The Mariner has not been released from pain at the moment the Albatross falls from him, nor is he admitted into Heaven, his sin forgiven: he has rather passed from the state of Hell (pain without purification) to the state of Purgatory (purifying penance).

The self-same moment I could pray;
And from my neck so free
The Albatross fell off, and sank   290
Like lead into the sea.

With the oncoming of grace, sleep comes. Sleep may be thought of as symbolic of the loss of self-concern, selfishness. If we equate beauty with grace, these lines from Keats' *Endymion* apply:

A thing of beauty is a joy forever:
Its loveliness increases; it will never
Pass into nothingness; but still will keep
A bower quiet for us, and a sleep
Full of sweet dreams, and health, and quiet breathing.

Bates (p. 27) comments on the word "silly." "The word first meant blessed, then innocent, then simple; finally foolishly simple. Here, empty, useless."

Rain is an ancient symbol of the purgation of the soul.

PART V

Oh sleep! it is a gentle thing,
Beloved from pole to pole!
To Mary Queen the praise be given!
She sent the gentle sleep from Heaven,   295
That slid into my soul.

By grace of the holy Mother, the ancient Mariner is refreshed with rain.

The silly buckets on the deck,
That had so long remained,
I dreamt that they were filled with dew;
And when I awoke, it rained.   300

When we wake up from a deep sleep, we are most susceptible to seeing the world differently. At such times the ordinary may seem strange. Lying in bed through an illness can also cause us to sense things differently.

The word "sere" is not logical here if we take it to mean dried up. Gardner (p. 76) directs us to a line from Captain Shelvocke's travel book: "Our sails were now grown so very thin and rotten." Shelvocke's report of his voyage was among the many travel books read by Coleridge.

My lips were wet, my throat was cold,
My garments all were dank;
Sure I had drunken in my dreams,
And still my body drank.

I moved, and could not feel my limbs: 305
I was so light—almost
I thought that I had died in sleep,
And was a blessèd ghost.

He heareth
sounds and
seeth strange
sights and
commotions
in the sky
and the ele-
ment.

And soon I heard a roaring wind:
It did not come anear; 310
But with its sound it shook the sails,
That were so thin and sere.

The aurora borealis is likened to a rebirth of the cosmos. Though the Mariner is still in a penitential state, the revitalization of the sky may be thought of as heralding his complete self-renewal.

"Sedge" is a coarse marsh grass.

We are reminded of our reference to Rossetti's line about the sighing of the soul. Now the sails seem to give back a mournful answer to the coming storm. The reader may think that the storm is the reproving voice of God.

The use of the word "fell" to describe the action of the lightning seems to be a less than satisfactory choice. It may stand up poetically but not scientifically.

The upper air burst into life!
And a hundred fire-flags sheen,
To and fro they were hurried about!   315
And to and fro, and in and out,
The wan stars danced between.

And the coming wind did roar more loud,
And the sails did sigh like sedge;
And the rain poured down from one black
    cloud;   320
The Moon was at its edge.

The thick black cloud was cleft, and still
The Moon was at its side:
Like waters shot from some high crag,
The lightning fell with never a jag,   325
A river steep and wide.

In his critical work, *The Enchanted Forest*, Werner W. Beyer makes an effective case for the position that Coleridge got his idea for his poem from the German narrative poem, *Oberon* by C. M. Wieland (1780). Beyer states in his preface, " . . . In *Oberon* Coleridge found what may be fairly called the missing map or key to Xanadu: found an unsuspected matrix or seven part circular pattern for *The Ancient Mariner* complete with theme of sin and penance and Second Birth."

With reference to this stage and to later stages of the *Rime*, Beyer (p. 93) writes: "From Part V to the end, . . . Wieland's sequence of . . . the sinner's experience of two aerial voices and daemonic propulsion in a trance, of a dream of joy and a vision of welcoming by some lovely lights, of mysterious return to his own country, and of his meeting with the hermit—seems to have continued to guide Coleridge's sensitively re-creating hand."

The bodies of the ship's crew are inspired and the ship moves on;

The loud wind never reached the ship,
Yet now the ship moved on!
Beneath the lightning and the Moon
The dead men gave a groan.

330

They groaned, they stirred, they all uprose,
Nor spake, nor moved their eyes;
It had been strange, even in a dream,
To have seen those dead men rise.

85

According to Wordsworth it was he who suggested that the resurrected dead men should work the ropes.

Commenting on "they raised their limbs like lifeless tools," and other such lines, H. D. Traill (p. 51) writes: " . . . everything seems to have been actually seen, and we believe it all as the story of a truthful eye-witness. The details of the voyage, too, are all chronicled with such order and regularity, there is such a diary-like air about the whole thing, that we accept it almost as if it were a series of extracts from the ship's log. Then again the execution—a great thing to be said of so long a poem —is marvelously equal throughout; the story never drags or flags for a moment, its felicities of diction are perpetual, and it is scarcely marred by a single weak line."

The helmsman steered, the ship moved on; 335
Yet never a breeze up-blew;
The mariners all 'gan work the ropes,
Where they were wont to do;
They raised their limbs like lifeless tools—
We were a ghastly crew.   340

The body of my brother's son
Stood by me, knee to knee:
The body and I pulled at one rope,
But he said nought to me.

"I fear thee, ancient Mariner!"   345
Be calm, thou Wedding-Guest!
'Twas not those souls that fled in pain,
Which to their corses came again,
But a troop of spirits blest:

But not by the souls of the men, nor by daemons of earth or middle air, but by a blessed troop of angelic spirits, sent down by the invocation of the guardian saint.

The sounds uttered by the dead men may call up in the reader's mind the idea of the souls of the men being offered up. The sounds blend with the songs of birds. The total effect is one of profound sweetness and naïveté. There is a childlike quality in these lines.

Traill (p. 47) writes: "One would not have said in the first place . . . that this was the man to have composed triumphantly at the very first attempt the terseness, vigour, and naïveté of the true ballad manner."

For when it dawned—they dropped their arms, 350
And clustered round the mast;
Sweet sounds rose slowly through their mouths,
And from their bodies passed.

Around, around, flew each sweet sound,
Then darted to the Sun; 355
Slowly the sounds came back again,
Now mixed, now one by one.

Sometimes a-dropping from the sky
I heard the sky-lark sing;
Sometimes all little birds that are, 360
How they seemed to fill the sea and air
With their sweet jargoning!

And now 'twas like all instruments,
Now like a lonely flute;
And now it is an angel's song, 365
That makes the heavens be mute.

This stanza, which is Wordsworthian in sound and subject matter, seems to be somewhat out of place.

The reader may imagine the giant hand of the Polar Spirit moving the ship almost like a toy.

It ceased; yet still the sails made on
A pleasant noise till noon,
A noise like of a hidden brook
In the leafy month of June,   370
That to the sleeping woods all night
Singeth a quiet tune.

Till noon we quietly sailed on,
Yet never a breeze did breathe:
Slowly and smoothly went the ship,   375
Moved onward from beneath.

Nine fathom deep would be fifty-four feet.

We are reminded of the earlier line, "painted ship upon a painted ocean." The ship has returned to the equator. The oscillation of the ship occurs as the forces of revenge (the Polar Spirit) contest with the forces of salvation (the angelic troop).

The lone-
some Spirit
from the
south pole
carries on the
ship as far as
the Line, in
obedience to
the angelic
troop, but
still requireth
vengeance.

Under the keel nine fathom deep,
From the land of mist and snow,
The spirit slid: and it was he
That made the ship to go.   380
The sails at noon left off their tune,
And the ship stood still also.

The Sun, right up above the mast,
Had fixed her to the ocean:
But in a minute she 'gan stir,   385
With a short uneasy motion—
Backwards and forwards half her length
With a short uneasy motion.

In making his case for paralleling Wieland's *Oberon* with Coleridge's *Mariner*, Beyer (pp. 94, 95) writes: "A vital cog in both the theme and the daemonic machinery of *Oberon*, . . . [Is the appearance of a chorus at the turning point and the hint of a method of dramatic compression] . . . by way of daemonic propulsion on the homeward leg of the circular voyage—a device which also appears in the *Rime* . . . Clearly in the *Mariner* for the time speaks Huon [the central character in *Oberon*], whose experience of daemonic propulsion and of two invisible voices we can watch in the very process of re-creation. The sublety and deftness with which Coleridge here selected and rewrought the fragments of *Oberon* seem almost uncanny."

Then like a pawing horse let go,
She made a sudden bound: 390
It flung the blood into my head,
And I fell down in a swound.

How long in that same fit I lay,
I have not to declare;
But ere my living life returned,   395
I heard and in my soul discerned
Two voices in the air.

The Polar Spirit's fellow-daemons, the invisible inhabitants of the element, take part in his wrong; and two of them relate, one to the other, that penance long and heavy for the ancient Mariner hath been accorded to the Polar Spirit, who returneth southward.

"Is it he?" quoth one, "Is this the man?
By him who died on cross,
With his cruel bow he laid full low   400
The harmless Albatross.

It will be helpful for the reader to return to John Ciardi's comments which were quoted at the end of Part IV.

The spirit who bideth by himself
In the land of mist and snow,
He loved the bird that loved the man
Who shot him with his bow." 405

The other was a softer voice,
As soft as honey-dew:
Quoth he, "The man hath penance done,
And penance more will do."

The image in this stanza pictures the reflected light of the moon upon the surface of the ocean as a kind of immense glittering eye. And surely the ocean should look upon the moon; they are natural partners!

It is difficult for us who live in an age of speed to appreciate the conception of speed they had in Coleridge's time. The poet very likely shared a common notion that excessive speed could not be tolerated by the human body.

PART VI

First Voice

"But tell me, tell me! speak again,   410
Thy soft response renewing—
What makes that ship drive on so fast?
What is the ocean doing?"

Second Voice

"Still as a slave before his lord,
The ocean hath no blast;   415
His great bright eye most silently
Up to the Moon is cast—

If he may know which way to go;
For she guides him smooth or grim.
See, brother, see! how graciously   420
She looketh down on him."

First Voice

The Mariner hath been cast into a trance; for the angelic power causeth the vessel to drive northward faster than human life could endure.

"But why drives on that ship so fast,
Without or wave or wind?"

Second Voice

"The air is cut away before,
And closes from behind.   425

With reference to the Mariner's trance, Lowes (p. 286) sees a parallel in *The Odyssey*: . . . "Ulysses is brought home to his native country ('Swiftly, swiftly flew the ship') in a trance." Lowes uses this passage from *The Odyssey*: " 'But now when bending to their work they tossed the water with their oars, upon Odysseus' lids deep slumber fell, sound and pleasant, very like to death . . . Safely and steadily [the swift ship] ran; no circling hawk, swiftest of winged things, could keep beside her. Running thus rapidly she cut the ocean waves, bearing a man of godlike wisdom, a man who had before met many griefs of heart . . . yet here slept undisturbed, heedless of all he suffered.' "

Fly, brother, fly! more high, more high!
Or we shall be belated:
For slow and slow that ship will go,
When the Mariner's trance is abated."

The super-
natural mo-
tion is re-
tarded; the
Mariner
awakes, and
his penance
begins anew.

I woke, and we were sailing on   430
As in a gentle weather:
'Twas night, calm night, the moon was high;
The dead men stood together.

All stood together on the deck,
For a charnel-dungeon fitter: 435
All fixed on me their stony eyes,
That in the Moon did glitter.

E. M. Tillyard (pp. 486–487) makes a case for viewing the poem as a spiritual adventure. It is the individual who is the philosopher, the poet, the artist who *"looks far forth"* and who also searches inward.

Tillyard writes: "The sea voyage, then, indicates spiritual adventure, as the ordinary journey or pilgrimage indicates the course of normal life. And it is not everyone who goes out of his way to seek adventure."

Tillyard then goes on to quote these lines from Coleridge's *Biographia Literaria,* xii: "The first range of hills, that encircles the scanty vale of human life, is the horizon for the majority of its inhabitants. On its ridges the common sun is born and departs. From them the stars rise, and touching them they vanish. By the many, even this range, the natural limit and bulwark of the vale, is but imperfectly known. Its higher ascents are

The pang, the curse, with which they died,
Had never passed away:
I could not draw my eyes from theirs   440
Nor turn them up to pray.

*The curse
is finally
expiated.*

And now this spell was snapt: once more
I viewed the ocean green,
And looked far forth, yet little saw
Of what had else been seen—   445

too often hidden by mists and clouds from uncultivated swamps, which few have courage or curiosity to penetrate. To the multitude below these vapours appear, now as the dark haunts of terrific agents, on which none may intrude with impunity; and now all aglow, with colours not their own, they are gazed at as the splendid palaces of happiness and power. But in all ages there have been a few who, measuring and sounding the rivers of the vale at the feet of their furthest inaccessible falls, have learned that the sources must be far higher and far inward; a few, who even in the level streams have detected elements which neither the vale itself nor the surrounding mountains contained or could supply. . . . It is the essential mark of the true philosopher to rest satisfied with no imperfect light, as long as the impossibility of attaining a fuller knowledge has not been demonstrated."

Like one, that on a lonesome road
Doth walk in fear and dread,
And having once turned round walks on,
And turns no more his head;
Because he knows, a frightful fiend   450
Doth close behind him tread.

But soon there breathed a wind on me,
Nor sound nor motion made:
Its path was not upon the sea,
In ripple or in shade.   455

It raised my hair, it fanned my cheek
Like a meadow-gale of spring—
It mingled strangely with my fears,
Yet it felt like a welcoming.

Gardner (p. 90) writes: "As the ship returns to the harbor, the Mariner sees the three objects—lighthouse, hill, church—in reverse order from which they were previously mentioned when the ship left the harbor."

As we continue to consider why the poet wrote as he did, this outcry makes us wonder about Coleridge's personal problem with sleeplessness. His addiction to opium tends to support the speculation that he spent many an hour in wearisome sleeplessness. If he were deprived of the needed narcotic, he might well have been trapped in such a state.

Swiftly, swiftly flew the ship,   460
Yet she sailed softly too:
Sweetly, sweetly blew the breeze—
On me alone it blew.

*And the
ancient Mar-
iner behold-
eth his native
country.*
Oh! dream of joy! is this indeed
The lighthouse top I see?   465
Is this the hill? is this the kirk?
Is this mine own countree?

We drifted o'er the harbour-bar,
And I with sobs did pray—
O let me be awake, my God!   470
Or let me sleep alway.

Beyer (p. 103) relates these stanzas to *Oberon*: "Huon saw a luminous scene: 'the moon mirrored in many a lake' as 'ever stiller grew . . . the realm of air.' Then the shimmering crimson palace seemed to rise, its gleam lighting up all the scene, and then appeared the many blessed spirits or shades 'in gleaming lily white,' immortal and as if angelic."

Robert Penn Warren sees the poem as containing two major themes: a primary theme relating to the imagination, and a secondary theme relating to a conscious religious interpretation. He writes (p. 248), "Suddenly, under the sweet breeze, the Mariner descries the home port. Appropriately, it is drenched in magnificent moonlight. But now we are to have another kind of light, too. By every corpse on deck stands a seraph-man with a body all of light by which the return is accomplished; the men of light [associated with the primary theme] and the moon [associated with the secondary theme], provide us with a final fusion of the imagination and the sacramental (religious) vision. We may, as it were, take them to be aspects of the same reality."

The harbour-bay was clear as glass,
So smoothly it was strewn!
And on the bay the moonlight lay,
And the shadow of the Moon.   475

The rock shone bright, the kirk no less,
That stands above the rock:
The moonlight steeped in silentness
The steady weathercock.

And the bay was white with silent light,   480
Till rising from the same,
Full many shapes, that shadows were,
In crimson colours came.

A little distance from the prow
Those crimson shadows were: 485
I turned my eyes upon the deck—
Oh, Christ! what saw I there!

Beyer (p. 103) continues: "Did Coleridge remember *Oberon*, 'like an angel o'er a tomb of death'?"

Gardner (p. 92) explains the term seraph-man: "In Christian mythology the highest order of angels, excelling all others in the fervor of their love, as distinguished from the cherubim, the second highest order, who excel in knowledge. Milton, in *Paradise Lost*, is believed to have been the first to shorten the word to 'seraph.'"

Each corse lay flat, lifeless and flat,
And, by the holy rood!
A man all light, a seraph-man,   490
On every corse there stood.

This seraph-band, each waved his hand:
It was a heavenly sight!
They stood as signals to the land,
Each one a lovely light;   495

This seraph-band, each waved his hand,
No voice did they impart—
No voice; but oh! the silence sank
Like music on my heart.

The reader may be tempted to think of the Pilot, his son, and the Hermit as a kind of metaphorical trinity. The Pilot may symbolize Man as the doer; he who is responsible for human progress. The boy might stand for Man in his innocence before the confrontation with evil. The Hermit may symbolize the retreat from life: the abnegation of self. The Mariner (Coleridge) then may be seen as the artist who gives expression to all this.

The idea of Man as a Pilot occurs in some unforgettable lines in George Bernard Shaw's *Man and Superman*. The devil says: "What is the use of knowing?" Don Juan answers: "Why, to be able to choose the line of greatest advantage instead of yielding in the direction of the least resistance. Does a ship sail to its destination no better than a log drifts no-whither? The philosopher is Nature's Pilot. And there you have our difference: to be in hell is to drift: to be in heaven is to steer."

"Shrieve"—to impose penance and to grant absolution. Shrove Tuesday was so named because it was a time for confession and absolution before Lent.

But soon I heard the dash of oars,   500
I heard the Pilot's cheer;
My head was turned perforce away
And I saw a boat appear.

The Pilot and the Pilot's boy,
I heard them coming fast: 505
Dear Lord in Heaven! it was a joy
The dead men could not blast.

I saw a third—I heard his voice:
It is the Hermit good!
He singeth loud his godly hymns   510
That he makes in the wood.
He'll shrieve my soul, he'll wash away
The Albatross's blood.

Two selections from Coleridge's other works may serve to clarify his image of the Hermit:

Aloof with hermit-eye I scan
The present work of present man—
A wild and dream-like trade of blood and guile,
Too foolish for a tear,
Too wicked for a smile.
    ["Ode to Tranquillity"]

Coleridge valued tranquillity and probably felt that the only way to achieve it was to retreat from the world. The Hermit is the symbol of that retreat.
And:

The good great man? Three treasures, love and light,
And calm thoughts, regular as infant's breath;—
And three firm friends, more sure than day or night,—
Himself, his Maker, and the angel Death.
    ["The Great Good Man"]

PART VII

The Hermit of the Wood,

This Hermit good lives in that wood
Which slopes down to the sea.   515
How loudly his sweet voice he rears!
He loves to talk with marineres
That come from a far countree.

He kneels at morn, at noon, and eve—
He hath a cushion plump: 520
It is the moss that wholly hides
The rotted old oak-stump.

The skiff-boat neared: I heard them talk,
"Why, this is strange, I trow!
Where are those lights so many and fair,   525
That signal made but now?"

Approacheth the ship with wonder.

"Strange, by my faith!" the Hermit said—
"And they answered not our cheer!
The planks looked warped! and see those
    sails,
How thin they are and sere!   530
I never saw aught like to them,
Unless perchance it were

115

Continuing in this vein, the reference to "owlet" may remind the reader of these powerful lines:

Forth from his dark and lonely hiding-place
(Portentous sight!) the owlet Atheism,
Sailing on obscene wings athwart the noon,
Drops his blue-fringèd lids, and holds them close,
And hooting at the glorious sun in Heaven,
Cries out, "Where is it?"
    ["Fears in Solitude"]

Brown skeletons of leaves that lag
My forest brook along;
When the ivy-tod is heavy with snow, 535
And the owlet whoops to the wolf below,
That eats the she-wolf's young."

"Dear Lord! it hath a fiendish look—
(The Pilot made reply)
I am a-feared"—"Push on, push on!" 540
Said the Hermit cheerily.

There has been some speculation as to the source of the rumbling sound. The reader may content himself with this reasoning: Coleridge was thinking that the sinking of a large vessel would be accompanied by tremendous rumbling sound. The water rushing in below decks might then be the sound the Mariner heard prior to the sinking.

The poet continues to portray the sight and sound of the sinking. The hill nearby echoes the sound.

The boat came closer to the ship,
But I nor spake nor stirred;
The boat came close beneath the ship,
And straight a sound was heard.   545

The ship suddenly sinketh.

Under the water it rumbled on,
Still louder and more dread:
It reached the ship, it split the bay;
The ship went down like lead.

The ancient Mariner is saved in the Pilot's boat.

Stunned by that loud and dreadful sound, 550
Which sky and ocean smote,
Like one that hath been seven days
      drowned
My body lay afloat;
But swift as dreams, myself I found
Within the Pilot's boat.   555

Upon the whirl, where sank the ship,
The boat spun round and round;
And all was still, save that the hill
Was telling of the sound.

H. D. Traill (pp. 52–53) writes: "With what consummate art are we left to imagine the physical traces which the mariner's long agony had left behind it by a method far more terrible than any direct description—the effect, namely, which the sight of him produces upon others—"

Martin Gardner's view (p. 100) may be more correct: "The Pilot shrieks because he had assumed the Mariner to be dead."

I moved my lips—the Pilot shrieked   560
And fell down in a fit;
The holy Hermit raised his eyes,
And prayed where he did sit.

I took the oars: the Pilot's boy,
Who now doth crazy go,   565
Laughed loud and long, and all the while
His eyes went to and fro.
"Ha! ha!" quoth he, "full plain I see,
The Devil knows how to row."

Martin Gardner (p. 102) writes: "Part of the Mariner's penance is to wander from land to land, periodically wrenched with agony until he finds a man to whom he can tell his ghastly tale—Lowes offers convincing evidence that Coleridge was strongly influenced here by two great legends of Christianity: the Wandering Jew and the Wandering of Cain." These medieval myths enjoyed considerable currency during Coleridge's time.

On the subject of the Hermit, Robert Penn Warren sees him as spanning both the imaginative theme and the religious theme (Priest of Nature and Priest of God). Warren goes on to write (p. 249): "The Hermit, however, has another aspect. He is also the priest of Society, for it is by the Hermit, who urges the Pilot on despite his fears, that the Mariner is received back into the world of men."

And now, all in my own countree,   570
I stood on the firm land!
The Hermit stepped forth from the boat,
And scarcely he could stand.

"O shrieve me, shrieve me, holy man!"
The Hermit crossed his brow.   575
"Say quick," quoth he, "I bid thee say—
What manner of man art thou?"

Forthwith this frame of mine was wrenched
With a woful agony,
Which forced me to begin my tale;   580
And then it left me free.

Since then, at an uncertain hour,
That agony returns:
And till my ghastly tale is told,
This heart within me burns.   585

I pass, like night, from land to land;
I have strange power of speech;
That moment that his face I see,
I know the man that must hear me:
To him my tale I teach.   590

The reader is struck with the complete change of mood here. Bates (p. 46) writes: "Observe the transition from the 'uproar' to the 'little vesper bell.'" After this the whole tone of the poem changes. This stanza is what, in music, would be called a modulating passage, changing key and subject.

What loud uproar bursts from that door!
The wedding-guests are there:
But in the garden-bower the bride
And bride-maids singing are:
And hark the little vesper bell,   595
Which biddeth me to prayer!

O Wedding-Guest! this soul hath been
Alone on a wide wide sea:
So lonely 'twas, that God himself
Scarce seemèd there to be.   600

A reason for Coleridge's use of the wedding here presents itself. His intention here may have been to compare erotic love (born of appetite) with the love of God (selflessness). The realization of life, therefore, grows from a wondering love for God and all that he has wrought. The Greek word for this form of love is "agape" (ah-gah-pay).

O sweeter than the marriage-feast,
'Tis sweeter far to me,
To walk together to the kirk
With a goodly company!—

To walk together to the kirk,   605
And all together pray,
While each to his great Father bends,
Old men, and babes, and loving friends
And youths and maidens gay!

Wordsworth lamented our failure in this regard:

Getting and spending, we lay waste our powers:
Little we see in Nature that is ours;
We have given our hearts away, a sordid boon!
The Sea that bares her bosom to the moon;
The winds that will be howling at all hours,
And are up-gathered now like sleeping flowers;
For this, for everything, we are out of tune;
It moves us not.—Great God! I'd rather be
A Pagan suckled in a creed outworn;
So might I, standing on this pleasant lea,
Have glimpses that would make me less forlorn;
  ["The World Is Too Much with Us"]

It moves us not? Apparently the Mariner's tale has moved the Wedding-Guest!

And to teach, by his own example, love and reverence to all things that God made and loveth.

Farewell, farewell! but this I tell   610
To thee, thou Wedding-Guest!
He prayeth well, who loveth well
Both man and bird and beast.

He prayeth best, who loveth best
All things both great and small;   615
For the dear God who loveth us,
He made and loveth all.

The Mariner, whose eye is bright,
Whose beard with age is hoar,
Is gone: and now the Wedding-Guest   620
Turned from the bridegroom's door.

He went like one that hath been stunned,
And is of sense forlorn:
A sadder and a wiser man,
He rose the morrow morn.   625

Famous Quotations

from *The Rime of the Ancient Mariner*

Lines 1-4

It is an ancient Mariner
And he stoppeth one of three.
"By thy long grey beard and glittering eye,
Now wherefore stopp'st thou me?"

Lines 7-8

"The guests are met, the feast is set:
May'st hear the merry din."

Lines 13-16

He holds him with his glittering eye—
The Wedding-Guest stood still,
And listens like a three years' child:
The Mariner hath his will.

Lines 21-24

"The ship was cheered, the harbour cleared,
Merrily did we drop

Below the kirk, below the hill,
Below the lighthouse top."

Lines 31-32

The Wedding-Guest here beat his breast,
For he heard the loud bassoon.

Lines 33-34

The bride hath paced into the hall,
Red as a rose is she;

Lines 53-54

And ice, mast-high, came floating by,
As green as emerald.

Lines 59-62

The ice was here, the ice was there,
The ice was all around
It cracked and growled, and roared and howled,
Like noises in a swound!

Lines 79-82

"God save thee, ancient Mariner!
From the fiends, that plague thee thus!—
Why look'st thou so?"—With my cross-bow
I shot the Albatross.

Lines 103-106

The fair breeze blew, the white foam flew,
The furrow followed free;
We were the first that ever burst
Into that silent sea.

Lines 117-118

As idle as a painted ship
Upon a painted ocean.

Lines 119-122

Water, water, everywhere,
And all the boards did shrink;
Water, water, everywhere,
Nor any drop to drink.

Lines 123-126

The very deep did rot: O Christ!
That ever this should be!
Yea, slimy things did crawl with legs
Upon the slimy sea.

Lines 127-128

About, about, in reel and rout
The death-fires danced at night;

Lines 157-161

With throats unslaked, with black lips baked,

We could nor laugh nor wail;
Through utter drought all dumb we stood!
I bit my arm, I sucked the blood,
And cried, A sail! a sail!

Lines 188-189

Is that a Death? and are there two?
Is Death that woman's mate?

Lines 190-194

Her lips were red, *her* looks were free,
Her locks were yellow as gold:
Her skin was as white as leprosy,
The Night-mare LIFE-IN-DEATH was she,
Who thicks man's blood with cold.

Lines 199-200

The Sun's rim dips; the stars rush out:
At one stride comes the dark;

Lines 232-235

Alone, alone, all, all alone,
Alone on a wide wide sea!
And never a saint took pity on
My soul in agony.

Lines 263-266

The moving Moon went up the sky,

And no where did abide:
Softly she was going up,
And a star or two beside—

Lines 292-293

Oh sleep! it is a gentle thing,
Beloved from pole to pole!

Lines 361-362

How they seemed to fill the sea and air
With their sweet jargoning!

Lines 369-372

A noise like of a hidden brook
In the leafy month of June,
That to the sleeping woods all night
Singeth a quiet tune.

Lines 514-518

This Hermit good lives in that wood
Which slopes down to the sea.
How loudly his sweet voice he rears!
He loves to talk with marineres
That come from a far countree.

Lines 560-563

I moved my lips—the Pilot shrieked
And fell down in a fit;

The holy Hermit raised his eyes,
And prayed where he did sit.

Lines 597-600

O Wedding-Guest! this soul hath been
Alone on a wide wide sea;
So lonely 'twas, that God himself
Scarce seemèd there to be.

Lines 614-617

He prayeth best, who loveth best
All things both great and small;
For the dear God who loveth us,
He made and loveth all.

QUESTIONS FOR DISCUSSION

1. Lines 4, 8, 12—Note expressions like "stopp'st," "May'st," "eftsoons," etc. What is the effect of this kind of language? What kind of atmosphere does it create? How does it add to the impact of the poem?

2. Line 13—With what sort of people or creatures do you associate a glittering eye?

3. Line 31—Is this line acceptable as a description of the Wedding-Guest's behavior? Can you improve on it? Check on the meaning of breast-beating.

4. Lines 33-34 and 190-193—Compare the description of the bride with the woman, Life-in-Death.

5. Lines 41-49—Which of these lines are most effective as a description of a ship in a stormy sea? Why?

6. Line 65—Why liken a sea bird to a human soul?

7. Line 76—Can an Albatross perch?

8. Line 81—We can only infer how the Mariner looked from the Wedding-Guest's question. Why is this effective?

9. Lines 93-102—Why were the crew members so subject to superstition? Are there any other callings in life which especially give rise to superstitious belief?

10. Lines 107-130—Why was the absolute calm of the sea worse than a storm? Which of these lines is most effective in conveying the poet's own image of the scene?

11. Line 125—What might Coleridge have had in mind when he referred to "slimy things"? Is he reaching too far?

12. Line 135—Coleridge offers a lengthy marginal

gloss at this point. What is your impression of his use of marginal glosses? Do they help you enjoy or understand the poem? Are they necessary?

13. Lines 143-146—The repetition of the word "weary" is mentioned in the commentary. Coleridge often repeats words, phrases, whole lines or stanzas. Explain how this adds to or detracts from the power of the poem.

14. Line 163—Compare the meaning of "agape" here with that given in the commentary at the end of the poem. Is there a relationship?

15. Line 174—Why does the sun appear to be broad?

16. Lines 172-180—At this point the commentary discusses Tillyard's thoughts on degrees of unreality. How does this work to draw the reader into the story?

17. Line 200—Is the commentary correct in its explanation for the suddenness of darkness at the equator?

18. Lines 210-211—Is the appearance of the star within the nether tip of the moon possible?

19. Lines 220-224—What are the teachings of the major religious faiths with respect to the existence and nature of the soul?

20. Line 230—At this point, Coleridge's gloss refers to "penance." What is penance?

21. Line 236—The commentary attempts to explain the use of the word "beautiful." What is your explanation?

22. Line 245—At this point the commentary takes a position relative to prayer. Defend or attack the position.

23. Lines 263-266—Examine the poet's gloss at this point. Has he added something to his original idea?

24. Line 282—Compare the earlier reference to "slimy things." Why the change? What is it that has changed?

25. Line 305—The commentary discusses the way we perceive things after a lengthy illness. Can you describe your personal experiences in this regard?

26. Line 325—What do you think about the verb, "fell"? Experiment with other words.

27. Line 327—Coleridge uses the word, "inspired" in the gloss. What does he mean? What do we mean when we use the word? What is interesting about the way the two meanings relate?

28. Lines 330-334—Why do the men rise from the dead?

29. Lines 350-362—What are the words which lend a childlike quality to these lines?

30. Lines 377-388—These lines require of the reader "that willing suspension of disbelief for the moment that constitutes poetic faith." Examine Coleridge's statement. Do you agree with the idea of poetic faith? Does poetic faith relate to religious faith?

31. Line 393—Read the gloss. Why must the Polar Spirit obey the angelic troop? Check the meaning of the word, "daemon."

32. Line 414—The commentary mentions the partnership of the ocean and the moon. Explain what is meant.

33. Line 435—What is a charnel-dungeon?

34. Line 442—Beginning at this point, the commentary quotes Tillyard and Coleridge at length. Can you evaluate yourself as to your own potential as a philosopher?

35. Line 468—At this stanza, the commentary mentions Coleridge's addiction to opium. Discuss the problem of addiction as you understand it.

36. Line 476—The commentary quotes Beyer, who wrote "A Matrix for the Ancient Mariner." What does matrix mean?

37. Line 501—With reference to the word "Pilot," the commentary quotes Shaw's line, "The philosopher is Nature's Pilot." Explain this line.

38. Line 517—Why might Coleridge's Hermit love to talk?

39. Line 536—Shelley referred to Coleridge as a

"hooded eagle among owls" when compared to other writers of the day. What did he mean?

40. Lines 546-550—The commentary attempts an explanation of the sound. What else might Coleridge have had in mind?

41. Line 560—Relate this situation to that referred to in Question 9.

42. Lines 578-581—Relate the Mariner's need to tell his tale to the therapy of confession. You may think in terms of the confessional used in the Roman Catholic Church, or in terms of the troubled individual who relates his problems to a psychiatrist. What are the similarities and differences? Is prayer a form of therapy?

43. Lines 605-609—To whom or to what might Coleridge be referring?

44. Lines 614-617—If Coleridge were to return to life in our day, would he feel that we are closer to carrying out the spirit of the Mariner's advice?

Individual Projects

1. Write a report on the Romantic period in English literature. Choose several major poets from the period. Select examples from their poems which illustrate the philosophy of the Romantic period.

2. Read Chapter XIV in Coleridge's *Biographia Literaria*. Select passages that seem significant to you and write a report in which you discuss your selections.

3. Assemble a representative body of critical commentary dealing specifically with *The Rime of the Ancient Mariner*. Take a position relative to the critical comments that seem most accurate or most worthwhile.

4. Prepare a dramatic reading of the poem. Attempt to make the characters come alive through the way you deliver the lines. You might even supply a musical background for the various parts of the poem.

5. Compare representative examples of the poems of Wordsworth and Coleridge. Take a position as to which was the finer poet. Defend that position.

6. Study another major poem by Coleridge. Discuss the impact and message of the poem.

7. Reread *The Rime of the Ancient Mariner*. Give examples of the poet's use of symbolism and imagery.

8. Read a biography of Coleridge and write a report in which you document your new insights into the poet as a human personality.

9. Read Oscar Wilde's *Ballad of Reading Gaol*. Compare this work with Coleridge's *The Rime of the Ancient Mariner*.

10. Read a book which contains the letters that

Coleridge wrote during his lifetime. Document the insights you have gained from this experience.

11. *The Rime* has been thought of as dreamlike. Analyze the poem, selecting those passages that seem most dreamlike. Explain why you made each selection.

12. Take a scene from *The Rime of the Ancient Mariner* and dramatize it. Memorize lines, action, etc. and present a fully realized performance.

13. Certain stanzas or sections of *The Rime of the Ancient Mariner* may particularly appeal to the student. Select those that appealed to you and explain your reasons for selecting them.

14. Read Robert Penn Warren's essay "A Poem of Pure Imagination: An Experiment in Reading." Write a summary of the essay.

15. Read Edgar Allan Poe's story, "The Black Cat." Compare the crimes in this story with the Mariner's crime. Write a paper in which you make this comparison, and in it discuss the problem of human perversity.

16. Certain events occur when the sun is on high. Others occur when the moon is shining. Write a paper in which you compare these events. What conclusions do you draw?

ADDITIONAL READING

Editions of Coleridge's Work

Poetry

Bates, H., Coleridge's *The Rime of the Ancient Mariner*, ed. with notes and introduction (New York, Longmans Green and Co., 1901).

Coleridge, E. H., *The Poems of Samuel Taylor Coleridge* (London, Oxford University Press, 1927).

Gardner, M., *The Annotated Ancient Mariner*, with introduction and notes (New York, Clarkson N. Potter, Inc., 1965).

Wordsworth and Coleridge, *Lyrical Ballads*, ed. with an introduction by R. L. Brett and A. R. Jones (New York, Barnes and Noble, 1963).

Prose

Coleridge, S. T., *Biographia Literaria*, ed. by J. C. Metcalf (New York, MacMillan, 1926).

Griggs, E. L., *Collected Letters of Samuel Taylor Coleridge* (London, Oxford University Press, Volumes I and II, 1956; Volumes III and IV, 1959).

Griggs, E. L., *Unpublished Letters of Samuel Taylor Coleridge*, Volumes I and II (New Haven, Yale University Press, 1933).

Poetry and Prose

Richards, I. A., *The Portable Coleridge*, ed. with an introduction (New York, Viking, 1950).

Biographical

Benet, L., *Coleridge, Poet of Wild Enchantment* (New York, Dodd Mead, 1952).

Chambers, E. K., *Samuel Taylor Coleridge, A Biographical Study* (London, Oxford University Press, 1938).

Hanson, L., *The Life of Samuel Taylor Coleridge: The Early Years* (New York, Russell and Russell, 1962).

Traill, H., *Coleridge* (English Men of Letters) (New York, Harper and Brothers).

Critical Studies

Beyer, W. W., *The Enchanted Forest* (Oxford, Basil Blackwell, 1963).

Ciardi, J., *How Does A Poem Mean?* (Boston, Houghton Mifflin, 1960).

Lowes, J. L., *The Road to Xanadu, A Study in the Ways of Imagination* (Boston and New York, Houghton Mifflin, 1927).

Ober, W. U., Burtness, P. S., and Seat, W. R., *Young Coleridge, Selected Source Materials* (Boston, D. C. Heath, 1963).

Warren, R. P., *Selected Essays, a Poem of Pure Imagination: An Experiment in Reading* (New York, Random House, 1958).

Anthologies

William, O., *Master Poems of the English Language*, with introduction by leading poets and critics of the English-speaking world; Tillyard, E. M. W., *Coleridge, The Rime of the Ancient Mariner*, pp. 483-488 (New York, Trident, 1966).

Bibliographical

Hoffman, H., *The Reader's Advisor* (New York, R. R. Bowker, 1964).

Kuntz, J. M., *Poetry Explication*, Revised Edition (Denver, Alan Swallow, 1962).

Audio-Visual Materials

Films

The Rime of the Ancient Mariner, 27 min., b & w, University of California Extension, Berkeley, California.

Records

Great Poets and Their Work: Samuel Taylor Coleridge, S 12″, 33⅓ RPM, Materials for Learning, Brooklyn, New York.

Forms of Poetry: The Rime of the Ancient Mariner, Side 1, 12″ 33⅓ RPM, Educational Audio-Visual, Pleasantville, New York.

Film Strips

The Ancient Mariner, J-S Modern Instructional Films, Illustrations taken from the engravings of Gustave Doré, 7015 "The Dreadful Deed," and 7016 "The Mariner Repents," Stanley Bowmar Co., Valhalla, New York.

Film Strips and Records

The Ancient Mariner 12″ 33⅓ RPM, read by Richard Burton (also "Kubla Khan" and "Frost at Midnight").

The Rime of the Ancient Mariner, film strip, Educational Record Sales, New York, N. Y.

Tapes

18th and 19th Century Poets and Poems of England: Samuel Taylor Coleridge, LG 65, Imperial Productions Inc., Kankakee, Illinois.